Conversational English for Spanish Speakers

Jane Flynn, Ph.D.
Cognitive Technologies
Minnesota City, MN 55959

Note to Students

After four years of high school and college Spanish I felt that I knew Spanish. But that confidence evaporated when, at the age of 19, I landed in Bolivia and had difficulty with everyday conversations.

Después de cuatro años de estudiar el idioma español, fui a Bolivia a la edad de 19 años, con confianza en mi habilidad de charlar en español. Pero esa confianza se evaporó al encontrar la negociación de la vida cotidiana.

What happened? Although I could understand Spanish, my speech was slow and non-automatic because I was reconstructing grammar lessons with every sentence. I was mentally choosing the right verb ending, deciding if a noun was masculine or feminine, getting the adjective in the right place, etc.

¿Qué me pasó? Aunque podía entender al español, mis respuestas fueran lentas porque estaba reconstruyendo lecciones de gramática con cada frase. Estaba mentalmente cogiendo el verbo correcto, decidiendo si un sustantivo era masculino o femenino, poniendo el adjetivo en el lugar proprio, etc.

Does this sound like your experience as an English learner? If so, this book is for you.

¿Quizás lo que me pasó parece igual a tu experiencia en aprender el inglés? Si es así, este libro es para ti.

Contents

Note to Students..2
Chapter 1: Hello and Goodbye.........................4
Chapter 2: Introducing People.......................12
Chapter 3: Talking About Family....................20
Chapter 4: Where Do You Live?.....................28
Chapter 5: Talking on the Phone...................36
Chapter 6: It's About Time..............................44
Chapter 7: Eating Out......................................52
Chapter 8: Talking About Friends..................60
Chapter 9: Free Time.......................................68
Chapter 10: Review Your Progress................76
Note to Teachers..80
Additional Resources......................................84
Dedication...86

Chapter 1: Hello and Goodbye

Listen to Conversations

Amy sees her neighbor, Mr. Turner.

Amy: Hello, Mr. Turner. How are you?

> Buenos días,
> Buenas tardes,
> Buenas noches,

Sr. Turner. ¿Cómo está usted?

Mr. Turner: I'm fine, thanks. How are you, Amy?

Estoy bien. Y tú, Amy, ¿cómo estás?

Your family is well?

La familia, ¿está bien?

Amy: My mom is fine, but my dad has a cold.

Mi mamá está bien, pero Papá tiene la gripe.

Mr. Turner: That's too bad. I hope he gets better soon.

¡Qué lastima! Ojalá que se mejore pronto.

Amy: Thanks. Well, I have to go now.

Muchas gracias. Bueno, tengo que irme.

Mr. Turner: Goodbye. Give my regards to everyone.

Adiós. Recuerdos a todos.

Amy meets her friend, Sam.

Amy: Hi, Sam. What's up? How are you?

    Hola, Sam. ¿Qué tal? ¿Cómo estás?

Sam: Fine, and you?

    Bien. ¿y tú?

Amy: I'm fine, but Leah has a cold.

    Estoy bien, pero Leah tiene la gripe.

Sam: Too bad. Hope she gets better soon.

    Lo siento. ¡Ojalá que se mejore pronto.

Amy: Thanks. How's your family?

    Gracias. Y tu familia ¿cómo está?

Sam: They're fine, thanks.

    Todos están bien, gracias.

Amy: Well, I have to go.

    Bueno, tengo que ireme.

Sam: Me too. See you later. Say hello to Leah for me.

    Yo también. Hasta luego. Recuerdos a Leah.

Amy: Be seeing you.

    Hasta la vista.

Learn Sentence Patterns

1. Hello, | Alexis | What's up? How are you?
   | Madison |
   ¡Hola! | Shawn | ¿Qúe tal? ¿Cómo estás?

2. I'm | fine. | bien.
   Estoy | o.k. | asi asi.
   | better. | mejor.
   | much better. | mucho mejor.

3. How are you, | Leah?
   ¿Cómo estás, | Sam?
   | Dr. Jones?
   ¿Cómo está usted, | Mrs. Moore?

5. How is | Sam? | He is fine.
   ¿Cómo está | Mr. Jones? | Está bien.

6. How is | Leah? | She is fine.
   ¿Cómo está | Amy? | Está bien.

7. How is | Alexis? | She is fine.
¿Cómo está | Miss Jones? | Está bien.
| Mr. Moore? |
| Martin? | He is fine.
Está bien.

8. How are | Alexis and Sam? | They are fine.
¿Cómo están | Mr. and Mrs. Turner? | Están bien.

9. Well, until | later. | luego.
Entonces, hasta | tomorrow. | mañana.
| tonight. | la noche.

10. Goodbye. Say hello to | everyone. | todos.
Adiós. Recuerdos a | your family. | la familia.
| Charo. | Charo.
| Joe and Eva. | José y Eva.

Practice Questions and Answers

1. Hello. How are you?
   I'm fine. And you?

2. Good morning. How are you, Anita?
   I'm fine. How are you, Mr. Smith?

3. How are Paul and Jenny?
   Paul's OK, but Jenny has a cold.

4. How's your family?
   They're fine, thank you.

5. Goodbye. Give my regards to your family.
   Goodbye, Mr. Smith. See you later.

6. Hi, Mike. What's up? How are you?
   I'm O.K. How's Leah?
   She's better, thanks. Well, I have to go now. See you later.

Practice with Partners

1. Hello, _____. How are you?

   I'm fine. And you?

   I'm _____ (fine, so so, better).

2. How is _____?

   He's fine, but _____ has a cold.

   She's fine, but _____ has a cold.

3. How are _____ and _____?

   They're fine.

4. Hi, _____. What's up? How are you?

   I'm fine. And you?

   I'm O.K. But I have a cold.

xxxxxxxxxxxxxxxxxxxxxxxxxxxxxxxxxxxxxxxxxxxxxxxx

TIP: Casi siempre, los norteamericanos responden "I'm fine" a la pregunta ¿Cómo estás?

No hay distintas formas de hablar con chicos a contraste a personas mayores. Es decir, no hay diferencias entre ¿Cómo estás? y ¿Cómo está usted?

Review: Reading Practice

1. Hello, Mr. Turner. How are you? How's your family?
   Hello, Alexis. I'm fine, but Shawn has a cold.
   Goodbye. Give my regards to your family.
   Goodbye, Alexis. See you tomorrow.

2. Hi, Mike. What's up? How are you?
   Hi, Jim. I'm so-so. I have a cold.
   That's too bad. Hope you feel better soon.
   Thanks, Jim. I have to go. See you this afternoon.
   Bye, Mike. See you later.

3. Hello, Jenny. How are you? How's Annie?
   Hello, Mrs. Moore. I'm fine, but Annie has a cold.
   I'm sorry. Hope she feels better soon.
   Thank you. Well, I have to go. See you later.
   Goodbye, Jenny. See you tomorrow.

4. Hi, Dan. What's up? How are you?
   I'm much better, thanks.
   Gotta go. See you this afternoon.

Check for Mastery

1. _____, ask _____ how | he / she | is.

2. _____, ask _____ how _____ and _____ are.

3. _____, tell _____ you will see | him / her | later. / tonight. / tomorrow.

4. _____, ask _____ and _____ how they are.

5. _____, say goodbye to _____ and ask | him / her | to give your regards to the family.

6. _____, tell _____ that you are feeling better. Ask how | he / she | is.

11

Chapter 2: Introducing People

Listen to Conversations

Mike meets two new kids at school

Mike: Hello, my name is Mike.
> Hola. Me llamo Miguel.

And you, what's your name?
> Y tú ¿cómo te llamas?

Matt: I'm Matt. And this is my friend Jim.
> Me llamo Mateo. Y éste es mi amigo Jaime.

Leah and Eva meet Leah's friend Gabby.

Leah: Gabby, this is my friend Eva.
> Gabriela, ésta es mi amiga Eva.

Gabby: Pleased to meet you.
> Mucho gusto.

Eva: Me, too.
> El gusto es mío.

As he leaves his new house, Mr. Turner meets his neighbor's daughter, Annie.

Mr. Turner: I'm Mr. Turner.

    Yo soy el señor Turner.

You're Sofia, aren't you?

    Tú eres Sofia, ¿verdad?

Annie: No, I'm Annie.

    No, yo soy Anita.

Mr. Turner: What's your last name?

    ¿Cuál es tu apellido?

Annie: My last name is Gomez.

    Mi apellido es Gómez.

Mike and Luke are talking

Luke: Say, what's that guy's name?

    Oye ¿cómo se llama ese chico?

Mike: His name's Will.

    Se llama Guillermo.

Luke: Do you know who that woman is?

    ¿Sabes quién es esa señora?

Mike: I think that's Mrs. Turner.

    Creo que es la señora Turner.

Learn Sentence Patterns

1. I am   Alexis.
   Yo soy Marcela.
           Leah.

2. You are Ella,   right?
   Tú eres Alex,   ¿verdad?
            Mia,

3. My last name is   Turner.
   Mi apellido es   Anderson.
                     Cummins.

4. My name is   Alexis.
   Me llamo   Shawn.
                Leah.

5. His last name is   Turner.
   Su apellido es   Cummins.

6. Her last name is | Hanson.
   | Payne.

   Su apellido es

7. What is | that man's   ese señor? | name?
   | that guy's   ese chico?
   | that woman's esa señora?
   | that girl's   esa chica?
   | that child's ese niño?
   | esa niña?

   ¿Cómo se llama

8. Alex, this is my friend | Paul.
   | Jack.
   | Abbie.
   | Sophia.

   Alex, éste es mi amigo

   Alex, ésta es mi amiga

9. That guy is | Luke, | right?
   | Dan, | ¿verdad?

   Ese chico es

10. That girl is | Leah, | right?
    | Danica, | ¿verdad?

    Esa chica es

Practice Questions and Answers

1. What is your name?

   My name is Stacey. What is your name?

   I'm Sofia.

2. What is your last name?

   My last name is Moore. What is your last name?

   My last name is Anderson.

3. That guy's name is Ben, right?

   No, he is Ethan. His last name is Brown.

4. Stacey, this is my friend Annie. Her last name is Brewton.

   Pleased to meet you. My last name is Smith.

5. That woman's last name is Brown, right?

   No, her last name is Turner.

6. That is Jon. Is his last name Bellock?

   Yes, it is.

Practice with Partners

1. Hello. What is your name?
   My name is _____. And you?
   I am _____.

2. What is your last name?
   My last name is _____ What is yours?
   My last name is _____.

3. What is that girl's name?
   Her name is _____.
   What is that boy's name?
   His name is _____.

4. This is my friend _____. Her last name is _____.
   This is my friend _____. His last name is_____.

5. That guy is _____. That girl is_____.
   That man's name is _____.
   That woman's name is _____.

Review: Reading English

1. Hello, My name is Gabby. My last name is Nelson. What is your name?

2. My name is Jonathan Payne. And this is my friend Paul. His last name is Turner.

3. That girl is Annie, right? What is her last name?

4. Good afternoon. My name is Dr. Flynn. What is your name?

5. Dr. Flynn, this is my friend Aiden. His last name is Anderson.

6. I have to go now. Say hello to Gabby and Ben. See you this afternoon.

    See you later.

7. Hello. I am Mia, and my last name is Clinton. What is yours?

    Pleased to meet you, Mia. I'm Eva, and my last name is Bellock.

Check for Mastery

1. _____, ask _____ what [his / her] name is.

   _____, tell [him / her] what your name is.

   Now, ask what [his / her] name is.

2. _____, ask _____ what [his / her] last name is.

   _____, tell ____ what your last name is. Ask [him / her] what [his / her] last name is.

3. _____, tell everyone your name. Then tell everyone what your last name is.

xxxxxxxxxxxxxxxxxxxxxxxxxxxxxxxxxxxxxxxxxxxxxxxx

Si es chico o hombre, "su nombre" = **his** name.

Si es chica o mujer, "su nombre" = **her** name.

Chapter 3: Talking About Family

Listen to Conversations

The teacher is talking to his new class

Mr. Lee: Do you have any brothers and sisters?
    ¿Tienes hermanos?

Emma: I have one brother and two sisters.
    Tengo un hermano y dos hermanas.
My brother is the oldest.
    Mi hermano es el mayor.
One of my sisters is older than me.
    Una de mis hermanas es mayor que yo.
The other is younger.
    La otra es menor.

Mr. Lee: How many brothers and sisters do *you* have?
    ¿Cuántos hermanos tienes tú?

Nathan: I have only one brother. His name is Carter.
    Tengo sólo un hermano. Se llama Carter.
He's eighteen years old.
    Tiene diez y ocho años.

Mr. Lee: Is he in college already?
    ¿Ya asiste a la universidad?

Nathan: No, he's still in high school.
    No, todavía está in el secondario.

Evelyn is talking about her family.

Evelyn: I have only one sister. Her name is Sarah.
Tengo sólo una hermana. Se llama Sara.
But we have two cousins here in this city.
Pero tememos dos primos en esta ciudad.
My cousin Michael has a little sister.
Mi primo Miguel tiene una hermanita.
She's only three years old.
Tiene sólamente tres años.

Chad is talking about his cousin Luke.

Chad: My cousin Luke is an only child.
Mi primo Luke es hijo único.
His parents are very nice.
Sus padres son muy simpáticos.
My uncle's name is Richard.
Mi tío se llama Ricardo.
But we call him Rick.
Pero lo llamamos Rick.
He's lots of fun.
Es muy divertido.

Claire introduces herself to the class.

Claire: Hello. My name is Claire. I am ten years old.
Hola. Me llamo Claire. Tengo diez años.
I have one sister. She is fifteen years old.
Tengo una hermana. Tiene quince años.

Learn Sentence Patterns

1. I have | two   dos | brothers.
   Tengo | three   tres | hermanos.
   | four   cuatro |
   | five   cinco |

2. I have | two   dos | sisters.
   Tengo | three   tres | hermanas.
   | four   cuatro |
   | five   cinco |

3. I have | two   2 | cousins.
   Tengo | three   3 | primos.
   | four   4 |
   | five   5 |
   | six   6 |
   | seven   7 |
   | eight   8 |
   | nine   9 |
   | ten   10 |

¿Cuántos años tiene

4. How old **is** **your brother?** tu hermano?
your sister? tu hermana?
your cousin? tu primo?

¿Cuántos años tienen **are** **your brothers?** tus hermanos?
your sisters? tus hermanas?
your cousins? tus primos?

5. My brother is

Mi hermano tiene

eleven	11
twelve	12
thirteen	13
fourteen	14
fifteen	15
sixteen	16
seventeen	17
eighteen	18
nineteen	19
twenty	20

years old.

años.

6

My brother Mi hermano	**is older** es mayor	**than me.** que yo.
My sister Mi hermana		
My brothers Mis hermanos	**are older** son mayores	
My sisters Mis hermanas		

Practice Questions and Answers

1. Do you have any brothers or sisters?
   I have two brothers and one sister.

2. Is your sister younger than you?
   No, she is older.

3. Are your brothers older or younger?
   One is older, and one is younger.

4. How old are you?
   I am twenty years old.

5. How old is your younger brother?
   He is fifteen.

6. How old is your older brother?
   He is twenty-two.

7. How many cousins do you have?
   I have ten cousins.

8. Is your cousin Miguel older or younger?

   He is younger than me.

9. How old are you?

   I am 20 years old. I am five years older than Miguel.

10. What is your sister's name? How old is she?

    Her name is Elena, and she is 12 years old.

11. What is your cousin's last name?

    His last name is Miller. He is younger than me.

12. How old is your cousin?

    He is only five years old.

13. How many brothers and sisters do you have?

    I don't have any brothers or sisters. I am an only child.

Practice with Partners

1. Do you have any brothers and sisters?

    I have _____ brothers and _____ sisters.

2. How old are you?

    I am _____ years old.

3. How old is your | brother / sister / cousin | ?

4. My | brother / sister / cousin | is _____ years old.

5. Is your | brother / sister / cousin | older than you?

6. Yes, | he / she | is older than me.

7. No, | he / she | is younger than me.

Check for Mastery

1. ____, ask ____ how many brothers and sisters [he / she] has.

2. ___, ask ____ if [he / she] has cousins.

3. ____, ask ___ how old [his / her] [brother / sister / cousin] is.

4. _____, say hello to _____. Ask what [his / her] last name is.
Now ask how old [he / she] is.

5. ____, tell _____ how many cousins you have. Ask [him / her] how many cousins [he / she] has.

Chapter 4: Where Do You Live?

Listen to Conversations

Anna and Maya are talking about where they live.

Anna: I live on Diversity Avenue. Where do you live?

Vivo en al avenida Diversity. Y tú ¿Dónde vives?

Maya: I live on Kedzie, number 3011.

Vivo en la calle Kedzie, número 3011.

Anna: What's your phone number?

¿Cuál es tu teléfono?

Maya: 346-9230.

tres, cuatro, seis--nueve, dos, tres, zero.

Anna: What street does your cousin live on?

¿En qué calle vive tu primo?

Maya: He doesn't live in Chicago anymore.

Ya no vive en Chicago.

He lives in a small town not far from here.

Vive en un pueblo no muy lejos de aquí.

Mike meets Joe and Adam

Mike: Hello. Where does your family live now?

¡Hola! ¿Dónde viven ahora?

Adam: We live on Fullerton Street now.

Ahora vivimos en la calle Fullerton.

Joe: Our house is near the school.

Nuestra casa queda cerca de la escuela.

Adam: Come see us anytime.

Nuestra casa es tu casa.

Mike: Thanks. I have to go now. See you later.

Gracias. Tengo que irme. Hasta luego.

Joe: See you soon.

Hasta pronto.

Annie asks Mr. Turner for directions

Annie: Hello, Mr. Turner. What's the church's address?

Buenos días, señor Turner. ¿Cuál es la dirección de la iglesia?

Mr. Turner: 210 Mill street. It's very close to the park.

La calle Molino, número 210. Queda muy cerca del parque.

Learn Sentence Patterns

¿Dónde vives?
¿Dónde viven

1. Where [do / does] [You / Alexis and Gabby / your cousins / Rob / Anita / your cousin] live?

¿Dónde vive

2. I live in [Vivo en]
 - New York.
 - Chicago.
 - Arizona.
 - Minnesota.
 - Saint Paul.
 - the country.

3. [He / Él / She / Ella] lives on [vive en]
 - Kedzie Avenue.
 - North Avenue.
 - Main Street.
 - campus.

4. Our | house casa / city ciudad / town pueblo / street calle / farm finca | is not very far from here.
   Nuestra … no está muy lejos de aquí.

5. | Elena / Connor / Gracie — lives (vive) / I — vivo / Michael and I / We — live (vivimos) / Jon and Ava / My brothers / My cousins — live (viven) | on Third Street
   en la calle Tercera.

6. | My mi / His / Her su / Their | address is 149 Devon Avenue.
   dirección es la Avenida Devon 149.

31

Practice Questions and Answers

1. Where do you live, Michael?
   On Third street, number 142.

2. What is your telephone number?
   507-482-3496.

3. Do you know Sarah's number?
   Yes, it's 608-592-6783.

4. Does your cousin live in a city?
   No, she lives on a farm.

5. Is your town very far from here?
   No, it's very close.

6. Where do you live, Teresa and Jim?
   We live in Madison, Wisconsin.

7. Where do Jon and Connor live?
   They live on campus.

Practice with Partners

1. Good morning, _____. Where do you live?
   I live ___ _____ (city).
   I live ___ _____ (street).

2. Is your house close to here?
   No, it is far.
   Yes, it is close.

3. What is your telephone number?
   It's _____.

4. Where do your cousins live?
   They live ___ _____ (city).
   They live ___ _____ (street).

5. Where do _____ and _____ live?
   They live in _____.

6. Where does _____ live?

   | He / She | lives in _____ on _____ | Street. / Avenue. |

7. Where do your friends live?

They live	on	North Avenue.
		campus.
	in	New York.

Review: Reading English

1. Good morning. My name is Mrs. Berg. I live on 5th Avenue in New York.

2. My name is Gracie. I live in Arizona on a farm. My cousins live in Minnesota.

3. Hello. My name is Martin. My last name is Weller. I live in Chicago. My address is 4944 Devon Avenue.

4. Good afternoon. My name is Anita. I live on a farm. It is very far from here.

5. Good evening. I am Marcela Martinez. I live in Bolivia. I live on Murillo Street in La Paz.

6. Hi. My name is Leah. Pleased to meet you. I live on campus. My telephone number is 450-5837.

7. Hello. My name is Anita. My family lives on a farm in Mexico. Now I live on campus. My telephone number is 608-779-2143.

8. Hello. My name is Dr. Flynn. I live in a small town.

Check for Mastery

1. _____, ask _____ where | he / she | lives.

2. _____, ask _____ if | her / his | house is far from here.

3. _____, say hello to _____ and ask where | he / she | lives.

4. _____, ask _____ if | he / she | lives on a farm.

5. _____, ask _____ for | her / his | phone number.

6. _____, ask _____ where | her / his | cousins live.

7. _____, ask _____ for the address of the school.

Chapter 5: Talking on the Phone

Listen to Conversations

Abigail calls the Flynn house to speak to Madison.

Mrs. Flynn: Hello.

¡Diga!

Abigail: Is Madison home?

¿Está en casa Madison?

Mrs. Flynn: Who's calling?

¿De quién hablo?

Abigail: Abigail Fox. I'm a friend of hers.

Abigail Fox, amiga suya.

Mrs. Flynn: Just a minute. I'll call her.

Un momento. Lo llamo.

Madison: Hello, Abby. What's up?

¡Hola! Abby. ¿Qué pasa?

Abigail: Want to go to a movie tonight? *Terminator II* is in town.

¿Quieres ir al cine esta noche? *Terminator II* está en el cine.

Madison: Sounds great. Maybe Adam and Evan would like to go with us?

> Me parece bien. ¿Quizás Adam y Evan les gustarían ir con nosotros?

Abigail: I'm going to see Adam now. I'll ask him.

> Voy a reunirme con Adam ahora. Le pideré.

Madison: Great. I'll pick you up at 7:30.

> Muy bién. Pasaré por ti a las siete y media.

Evan is talking to his friend Adam on the phone.

Evan: Hi, Adam. How are you? Doing anything tonight?

> ¡Hola! Adam. ¿Qué tal? ¿Tienes esta noche libre?

Abby and Madison are going to the movies tonight.

> Abby y Madison van al cine esta noche.

Want to go with them? The movie is *Terminator II*.

> ¿Quieres ir con ellas? La película es *Terminator II*.

Adam: Sounds good. I heard it´s a good movie.

> Me parece bien. He oído que es una pelicula buena.

Evan: I'll tell them we'll meet at eight.

> Les diré que nos esperen a las ocho.

Adam: Good. See you later.

> Bueno. Hasta luego.

Practice Sentence Patterns

1. Good morning. May I speak with | Dr. Smith?
   Buenos días. ¿Favor de hablar con | Mr. Nelson?
   | the principal?
   | the director?

2. Hello. Is | Sofia | there?
   ¡Hola! Está | Alex | en casa?
   | Will |

3. Hi, | Joe. | What's new?
   Hola, | Megan. | ¿Qué pasa?
   | Tom. |
   | Pete. |

4. Hello. Is this | Stacey's | house?
   Hola. ¿Es ésta | Annie's | la casa de _____?
   | Luke's |

5. Tell them to meet us at | seven thirty.   7:30
   Díles que nos esperen a las | nine fifteen.   9:15

38

6. I heard that the [movie / store / cafe / program] is very good.

He oído que la [película / tienda] es muy buena.

He oído que el [café / programa] es muy bueno.

7. Maybe your [cousin / brother / cousins / brothers] would like to go with us?

¿Quizás tu [cousin / brother] le gustaría ir con nosotros?

¿Quizás tus [cousins / brothers] les gustarían ir con nosostros?

8. They will meet us at the [movie. / store. / cafe. / program.]

Nos esparemos a la [película. / tienda.]

Nos esparemos al [café. / programa.]

9. Hi, Adam. Do you want me to call [Alex / Cindy / your friends / Jim and Lily] ?

Hola, Adam. ¿Quieres que le llame a [Alex / Cindy] ?

Hola, Adam. ¿Quieres que les llame a [your friends / Jim and Lily] ?

39

Practice Questions and Answers

1. Hello. Is Ben home?

    No, he's not. I'll tell him you called.

2. Hello, Amelia. What's new?

    Abbie and Char are going to the movies tonight. Do you want to go with them?

3. Do you want to go to a restaurant tonight?
    Sounds good. I'll pick you up at 6:00.

4. Hello. Can I talk to Logan?

    He's not here. Who's calling, please?

    Lily. Tell him I will meet him on campus at 3:00.

5. Hello, Mike. Are you free tonight?

    Yes, would you like to go to the movies?

6. Would Leah like to go to the program with us today?

    I will see her this afternoon. I'll ask her.

7. Tell Emily and Leah to meet us at 4:30 to go to a restaurant.

    Sounds good. See you later.

Practice with Partners

1. Hello, _____. Is _____ home?

   No, | he / she | is at the store.

   Tell | him / her | to call me when | he / she | gets home.

2. _____, do you want to go to | a show / a movie / the café / the library | tonight?

No, thanks. I have a cold.
I'm going to stay home tonight.

3. I hope you feel better soon.

   Thanks. See you later.

4. Hello, _____. Is _____ home?

   | No, / Yes, | I'll tell | him / her | you called.

Review: Read and Respond

Lupe is at the home of her friend, Olivia. They want to go to a movie. Lupe said the movie, *Terminator II,* is very good. They will meet Eva and Lily at seven o'clock.

    1. Where is Lupe?

    2. What do Lupe and Olivia want to do?

    3. What is the name of the movie?

    4. What did Lupe say about the movie?

    5. When will they meet Eva and Lily?

Mr. Nelson calls his brother from the airport. He is in New York. He wants to get home to Chicago tonight. The plane will be there at eight o'clock. He asks his brother to meet him at the airport.

    1. Where is Mr. Nelson?

    2. Who does he call?

    3. Where is his home?

    4. When will he get home?

    5. What does he ask his brother to do?

Check for Mastery

1. _____, call _____ and ask [him/her] if _____ is home.

2. _____, tell _____ that your [brother/sister] is not home.

3. _____, ask _____ what's up. What does [he/she] want to do tonight.

4. _____, tell _____ that your friends _____ and _____ are going to a restaurant tonight.

5. _____, call _____ to tell [him/her] that the movie tonight is _____.

6. _____, tell _____ that the movie tonight is _____. Tell [him/her] that it's [very good. / not very good.]

43

Chapter 6: It's About Time

Listen to Conversations

Tony, Jon and Max are waiting for the bus.

Tony: What time is it?

    ¿Qué hora es?

Max: I have 8:30.

    Según mi reloj, son las ocho y media.

Tony: The bus is late. We're going to be late for school.

    El bús anda atrasado. Vamos a llegar tarde a la escuela.

Jon: My watch says 8:15.

    Según mi reloj, son las ocho y quince.

Max: Then my watch is fast.

    Entonces mi reloj anda de prisa.

Jon: Look. Here comes the bus now.

    ¡Mira! Ya viene el bús.

Sarah and Haley are talking in the hall

Sarah: What time do you leave home in the morning?

    ¿A qué hora sales de casa por la mañana?

Haley: I leave the house at 8:00. The bus comes at 8:10. I get here around 8:30.

   Salgo a las ocho. El bús llega a las ocho y diez. Llego aquí como a las ocho y media.

Sarah: Do you eat at twelve or twelve thirty?

   ¿Comes a las doce o doce y media?

Haley: I usually eat at one o'clock, but today I'm eating at twelve.

   Generalmente como a la una, pero hoy voy a comer a las doce.

Sarah: Me too. It´s ten minutes to twelve. Let's go eat.

   Yo también. Faltan sólo diez minutes. ¡Vámanos!

Sophie and Connor are talking after school.

Connor: When do you want to go to the movies?

   ¿Cuándo quieres ir al cine?

Sophie: There's a show at 4:00 today. Cindy told me that it's very good.

   Hay una película a las cuatro hoy. Cindy me dijo que es muy buena.

Connor: How close to 4:00 is it now?

   ¿Cuánto falta para las cuatro?

Sophie: Just 30 minutes. Let´s go.

   Faltan sólo treinta minutos. Vámanos.

Practice Sentence Patterns

Según mi reloj, es la
1. According to my watch, it's
Según mi reloj, son las

one o'clock.	1:00
one thirty.	1:30
two fifteen.	2:15
quarter to three.	2:45
ten to four.	3:50

2. Then my watch is

Entonces mi reloj anda

slow.	atrasado.
fast.	adelantado.
a little slow.	un poco atrasado.

3. Tom is coming here

Tomás viene aquí

at one o'clock.	a la una.
at five o'clock.	a las cinco.
at noon.	al mediodía.
in the afternoon.	por la tarde.

4. We'll get together
   Nos vemos

later.	luego.
Monday.	el lunes.
at two o'clock.	a las dos.

5. When do you
   ¿A qué hora

leave your house?	sales de casa?
catch the bus?	tomas el bús?
eat lunch?	almuerzas?
have to be home?	tienes que estar en casa?

6. When do you want to
   ¿Cuándo quieres

eat?	comer?
go to the movies?	ir al cine?
leave here?	salir de aquí?
eat lunch?	almorzar?

7.

Mary	eats	come	
Luke			
I	eat	como	at two o'clock.
John and I	eat	comemos	
We			
Annie and Lisa	eat	comen	
My parents			
My friends			

Practice Questions and Answers

1. What time is it?

   It's 12:00. Time for lunch.

2. Is it two o'clock yet?

   Yes. According to my watch, it's a minute after two.

3. How long is the movie?

   Two and a half hours.

4. When do you eat breakfast at your house?

   We eat at eight thirty.

5. What time do you have?

   It's four o'clock.

6. Do you want to go to the store this afternoon?

   No, let's go this evening.

7. When does your family eat dinner?

   We eat at seven o'clock.

Practice with Partners

Sylvia and Gabby meet after class.

Sylvia: Do you want to go to a movie this afternoon?

Gabby: I don't know. How long is it?

Sylvia: About two hours. They say it's very good.

Gabby: O.K. I think I have time.

Sylvia: What time do you need to be back on campus?

Gabby: We eat at seven o'clock, so I have time to go to an afternoon movie.

Rob and Tom are waiting for the bus.

Rob: What time do you have?

Tom: According to my watch, it's eight fifteen.

Rob: Here comes the bus. Where's Paul? He's usually early.

Tom: Look. He's coming now.

Rob: Hurry up, Paul. The bus is leaving now.

Review: Writing About Time of Day

Directions: Write about your day.

    When do you get up?

    When do you eat breakfast?

    At what time do you go to class?

    When do you eat lunch?

    What do you do after class?

    What do you do in the evening?

Check for Mastery

1. _____, ask _____ when | he / she | eats lunch.

2. _____, say hello to _____. Ask | him / her | what time it is.

3. _____, ask _____ if | he / she | wants to go to the store.

4. _____, ask _____ and _____ if they want to go to the movies.

5. _____, ask _____ and _____ if they want to play soccer this afternoon.

6. _____, tell _____ that the bus is coming. | He / She | needs to hurry up.

7. _____, ask _____ if | he / she | wants to go to the movie tonight.

Chapter 7: Eating Out

Listen to Conversations

Sam and Eva meet on the campus mall.

Sam: Don't you ever eat in the cafeteria?

    ¿No comes nunca en la cafetería?

Eva: No, because the food is bad.

    No, porque la comida es mala.

Sam: You're right. It's awful.

    Tienes razón. ¡Malísimo!

Eva: I don't like vegetables.

    A mí no me gustan las legumbres.

Sam: Neither do I.

    Tampoco a mí.

Eva: Let's go to that new restaurant today.

    Vámanos al restaurante nuevo hoy.

Sam: Sorry, I can't. I have to study for a test.

    Lo siento, no puedo. Tengo que estudiar para un exámen.

Olivia and Evelyn are eating at a restaurant

Olivia: This restaurant looks really good!
   ¡Este restaurante se ve bien!

Evelyn: I'm really hungry!
   ¡Qué hambre tengo!

Olivia: I ordered chicken and rice. It's my favorite.
   Pidí arroz con pollo. Es mi favorito.

Evelyn: A steak for me.
   Para mí, un filete.

Olivia: Pass the salt and pepper, please.
   Pásame la sal y pimiento, por favor.

Evelyn: Look. I don't have a knife.
   ¡Mira! Me falta el cuchillo.

Olivia: Take mine. I don't need it.
   Tome el mío. No lo necesito.

As the girls finish, the waiter comes to their table.

Waiter: Would you like a desert?
   ¿Desean algo de postre?

Evelyn: No, thanks. The check, please.
   No, gracias. La cuenta, por favor.

Learn Sentence Patterns

Me gusta este/a	restaurant.	restaurante.
1. I like this	meal.	comida.
	breakfast.	desayuno.
	lunch.	almuerzo.
	dinner.	cena.

Pásame	salt,	la sal,	
2. Pass the	pepper,	el pimiento,	por favor.
	cheese,	el queso,	please.
	bread,	el pan,	
	butter,	la mantequilla,	

3. Do you like	ham?	el jamón?
¿Te gusta	milk?	la leche?
	soup?	la sopa?
	dessert?	el postre?
	chicken?	el pollo?
	vegetables?	los vegetales?
¿Te gustan	eggs?	los huevos?

4. I don't like
No me gustan
No me gusta

vegetables.	las verduras.
salads.	las ensaladas.
lamb.	el cordero.
rice.	el arroz.

5. I don't have a
Me falta

fork.	el tenedor.
spoon.	la cuchara.
glass.	el vaso.
menu.	el menú.
napkin.	la servilleta.
knife.	el cuchillo.

6. This ... **is delicious.**
Este ... *está delicioso.*
Esta ... *está deliciosa.*

lamb	cordero
rice	arroz
steak	filete
soup	sopa
fruit	fruta

7. Please bring me
Favor de traerme

French fries.	papas fritas.
tomato soup.	sopa de tomate.
a steak.	un filete.
the bill.	la cuenta.

Practice Questions and Answers

1. What would you like, Dr. Mendoza?
   I'd like a steak, please.

2. What would you like, Alex?
   I'd like some rice and beans.

3. How is the chicken and rice?
   It's delicious. Would you like some?

4. Mary, I don't have a spoon.
   Take mine. I don't need one.

5. Do you like the food in the cafeteria?
   Sometimes, but we have a lot of rice and potatoes.

6. Do you like vanilla or chocolate ice cream?
   Neither. I like fruit for dessert.

7. Would you like to go to the new restaurant today?
   Sounds good. I'll pick you up at 6:00.

Practice with Partners

1. Does _____ like the food in the cafeteria?

   No, | he | likes   MacDonald's.
       | she |

2. Hello, _____. Is it time for lunch yet? When do you eat?

   No, it's 11:15. I eat at 12:00. Would you like to go to the cafeteria with me?

   What's for lunch today?

   I think it's eggs and ham.

   Then I want to eat at MacDonald's today.

3. _____, when does your family eat dinner?

   They eat at 7:00. But I come home later. I have classes until 7:30. When do you eat dinner?

   My family eats at 6:00 and then I study for my classes.

4. _____, do you want to go out to eat tonight?

   Sorry, I have to study for a test tomorrow.

   See you tomorrow, then.

   See you later.

Review: Read and Respond

Abbie and Sofia are downtown eating dinner before going to a movie. Sofia orders steak with French fries. Abbie orders rice with vegetables. The waiter asks if they would like dessert. Neither of the girls order dessert. They want to see "Frozen" and it starts in five minutes, so they need to hurry. The waiter brings them the check, and they run down Main Street to the movie theater.

1. Where are Abbie and Sofia?
2. What are they doing?
3. What does Abbie order to eat?
4. Why don't they eat dessert?
5. What movie do they want to see?
6. When does it start?

Jim and Mason go to the cafeteria to see what is on the menu today. It is ham and cheese, and neither student likes that. They talk about going to MacDonald's to eat. But they decide to go to the new restaurant in town, the Acoustic, because there is good food and music every night.

1. What is on the cafeteria menu today?
2. Why don't Jim and Mason want to eat there?
3. Where do they go to eat?
4. Why do they go there to eat?

Check for Mastery

1. _____, ask _____ if [he / she] likes vegetables.

2. _____, tell [him / her] that you don't like vegetables. You like French fries.

3. _____, tell _____ that you don't have a spoon. Ask if [he / she] has an extra one.

4. _____, ask _____ if [he / she] likes MacDonald's or Burger King better.

5. _____, tell ____ when your family eats dinner. Ask when [his / her] family eats dinner.

6. _____ and _____, tell each other what your favorite foods are. Now tell each other what you don't like to eat.

Chapter 8: Talking About Friends

Listen to Conversations

Emily and Harper are chatting between classes.

Emily: Do you know that guy?

¿Conoces a ese chico?

Harper: Yes. His name is Luke. He's a nice guy. Also very smart.

Sí. Se llama Luke. Es un chico muy simpático. También muy listo.

Emily: Who is that girl with him? Is she his girlfriend?

¿Quién es la chico con él? ¿Son novios?

Harper: No, that's his sister. She's younger than him. Her name is Isabella.

No, es su hermana. Es menor que él. Se llama Isabela.

Harper: What's she like?

¿Cómo es?

Emily: She's very nice also. Would you like to meet them?

Es muy simpática también. ¿Quieres conocerles?

Eva and Jim are leaving the movie.

Eva: Look. There's Olivia.

    Mira, aquí viene Olivia.

Jim: I don't know her.

    No la conozco.

Eva: Really? She's Ben's older sister. She's very smart.

    ¿De veras? Es la hermana mayor de Ben. Es muy lista.

Olivia: Hi, Eva. How are you? What's up?

    ¡Hola! Eva. ¿Cómo estás? ¿Qué hay de nuevo?

Eva: I'm fine. Olivia, I'd like you to meet my friend, Jim.

    Estoy bien. Olivia, me gustaría que conocieras a mi amigo, Jim.

Eva: Hello, Jim. Glad to meet you.

    Hola, Jim. Mucho gusto.

Jim: Likewise. You're Ben's sister, right? He's a good friend of mine.

    Lo mismo. Eres hermana de Ben ¿verdad? Es muy amigo mío.

Olivia: Really? He's coming to visit next week. I'll tell him I met you today.

    ¿De veras? Viene a visitarme la semana que viene. Le diré que te conocí hoy.

Learn Sentence Patterns

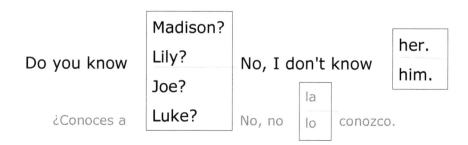

5. Lily and Ana are two very [smart listas. / nice simpáticas.] girls.
   Lily y Ana son dos chicas muy

6. Are [Ava and Joe / Mia and Luke / Sofia and Dan] [dating? novios? / friends? amigos?] No los conozco. I don't know them.
   ¿Son

7. I don't know [Ava. / Mia. / Dan. / Luke.] Do you know [her? / him?]
   No conozco a ... [¿La / ¿Lo] conoces tú?

8. Kyle, I'd like you to meet my friend [Mia. / Dan.]
   Kyle, me gustaría que conocieras a mi [amiga / amigo]

9. Who are those [guys? esos chicos? / girls? esas chicas?]
   ¿Quiénes son

10. I don't know them. No [los / las] conozco.

Practice Questions and Answers

1. Kyle, do you know my friend Madison?
   No, I don't know her. What's she like?
   She's very nice. And smart, too.

2. Jim, I'd like you to meet my friend, Harper.
   Pleased to meet you, Harper.

3. Who are those two guys?
   That's Ben and Logan. They're friends of mine.

4. Are Eva and Kyle sweethearts?
   No, they're just friends. Kyle is dating Jen.

5. Do you know Hannah and Abbie?
   Yes, we are good friends.

6. What is Ellen like?
   She's very nice and very funny. She's also very smart.

Practice with a Partner

1. _____, do you know _____?
   Yes, | he / she | is a friend of mine.

2. _____, please introduce me to your friend _____.
   _____, this is my friend _____.

3. Who are those | guys? / girls? | I don't know them.
   They are ___ and ____. We are very good friends.

4. _____, I'd like you to meet my friend _____.
   Glad to meet you. Are you friends with _____?
   No, | he / she | is my | brother. / sister.

5. _____, are you and _____ dating?
   No, we are just friends.

Review: Read and Respond

Leah and Michael are dating. They go to the movie to see "Frozen." Leah thinks that it is very good, but Michael thinks it's bad. After the movie, they meet their friend, Lily. Lily thinks that the movie was very funny.

1. Are Leah and Michael sweethearts or just friends?
2. Where do they go?
3. What's the name of the movie?
4. What does Leah think about the movie?
5. What does Michael say about the movie?
6. Who do they meet after the show?

Ben and Abbie are talking in the cafeteria. Ben sees two girls that he does not know coming in. He asks Abbie who they are. Abbie tells him that they are her friends Harper and Sofia.

1. Where are Ben and Abbie?
2. What does Ben ask Abbie?
3. Who are the two girls coming in?
4. What does Abbie tell him about Harper and Sofia?

Check for Mastery

1. _____, ask _____ who that guy over there is.
   _____, tell [him/her] that he is your friend _____,

2. _____, introduce your friend _____ to _____.
   ___, tell _____ that you are pleased to meet [him./her.]

3. _____, ask _____ if _____ and _____ are dating.
   _____, tell [him/her] that they are just friends.

4. _____, ask _____ if [he/she] knows _____ and _____.
   _____, tell [him/her] that you don't know them.

5. _____, introduce your friend _____ to _____.

Chapter 9: Free Time

Haley and Alexis are leaving the cafeteria.

Haley: What are you doing tonight?

¿Qué piensas hacer esta noche?

Alexis: Not much. Study a little, check out Facebook, chat with my friends.

Más or menos nada. Estudiar un poco, checkear el Facebook, charlar con mis amigas.

Haley: I have a Biology test tomorrow. I have to study a lot.

Tengo un exámen de Biología mañana. Tengo que estudiar mucho.

Alexis: My test is next week. I have to write a paper for English.

Mi exámen está la semana que viene. Tengo que escribir un ensayo por Inglés.

Haley: Well, I'll see you tomorrow.

Pues, hasta mañana.

Alexis: See you later. Good luck on your exam!

Hasta luego. ¡Éxito en el exámen!

Haley: Thanks. I'll call you later.

Gracias. Te llamo más tarde.

Jacob and Liam are studying for a test.

Jacob: This textbook is really hard. I need a break. Want to watch television?

> Este texto es muy difícil. Necesito tomar un descanso. ¿Quieres ver la televisión?

Liam: Anything good on tonight?

> ¿Hay algo bueno esta noche?

Jacob: *Adventure Time* is on in thirty minutes.

> *Hora de Aventura* empieza en treinta minutos.

Liam: I've heard it's pretty funny.

> He oído que es muy divertido.

Jacob: Yes, I'm sure you'll like it. Lots of jokes.

> Sí. Te gustará, sin duda. Muchos chistes.

Liam: What's it about?

> ¿De que se trata?

Jacob: It's a cartoon series about Jake the Dog and Finn the Human. They have a lot of fun adventures.

> Es un serie de dibujos animados sobre Jake el Perro y Finn el Humano. Tienen un montón de aventuras divertidas.

Jacob: Sounds good. Let's study for fifteen minutes more, then take a break to watch television.

> Me parece bién. Estudiémos quince minutos más, y entonces tomemos un descanso para ver la televisión.

Liam: O.K. Let's review the vocabulary terms one more time.

> Bueno. Revisemos el vocabulario una vez más.

Learn Sentence Patterns

1. Would you like to | Play Pokémon GO / jugar a Pokémon GO / go to a football game / ir al juego de fútbol | now? / ahora?
   ¿Quisieras

2. What are you going to do | tonight? esta noche? / this afternoon? esta tarde? / this weekend? este fin de semana? / tomorrow? mañana?
   ¿Qué piensas hacer

3. Today I'm planning to | listen to music. escuchar a la música. / play tennis. jugar al tenis. / go downtown. ir al centro.
   Hoy pienso

4. I don't like | that TV station. esa estación de TV. / that book. ese libro. / concerts. conciertos. / political magazines. revistas políticas.
   No me gusta / No me gustan

5. Come to my house

    Vente a mi casa

Sunday.	el domingo.
Monday.	el lunes.
Tuesday.	el martes.
Wednesday.	el miércoles.
Thursday.	el jueves.
Friday.	el viernes.
Saturday.	el sábado.

6. Let's go to the movies

    Vámanos al cine

Sunday.	el domingo.
this Friday.	este viernes.
later.	más tarde.
tonight.	esta noche.

7.

I	am *Estoy*	
Luke		
Shelley	is *está*	playing cards.
Joe and I	are	*jugando a las cartas.*
We	*estamos*	
My cousins	*están*	
My friends		

Practice Questions and Answers

1. When should I come to your house tonight?

    At 8:00. We can study a little and then watch TV.

2. Anything good on TV tonight?

    The Packers are playing the Vikings.

3. Which team is your favorite?

    I live in Minnesota. I'd like the Vikings to win.

4. Would you like to go to the movies tomorrow night?

    Yes. Lily and Ava are going, too. Let's meet them.

5. When should we meet them?

    The movie starts at seven. Let's meet them at 6:30.

6. What do you want to do after class?

    Let's go downtown. I want to shop for shoes.

7. What is this TV show about?

    It's a cartoon story about a dog and a human.

Practice with a Partner

1. Hello, _____. What are you doing tonight?
   I'm going to _____. And then I will _____.

2. _____, do you want to go to the movies tonight?
   No, I have to _____. Let's go _____.

3. Hi, _____. What's up? Do you like the food today?
   No, the cafe food is always bad. I don't like _____.

4. Hello, _____ what book are you reading now?
   I'm reading _____. It's very _____

5. _____, do you like the _____ TV station?
   Yes, it has good _____.

6. _____, what is your favorite movie?
   I like _____. I watched it on Netflix last night.

7. _____, What are you doing this weekend?
   I'm going downtown to shop for a new dress.

Review: Read and Respond

Rob, Eva and Jon are studying for a history test tomorrow. Eva says that she needs a break. Rob says that the football game between the Packers and Vikings is on TV tonight. Jon likes the Packers because he is from Wisconsin. Eva and Rob are from Minnesota, so they like the Vikings.

1. What are the three friends doing?
2. Who says that he/she needs a break?
3. What does Rob say about TV?
4. Why does Jon like the Packers?
5. Why do Eva and Rob like the Vikings?

Shelley and Jenny are downtown shopping for dresses for the concert next week. They heard that the new restaurant, the Acoustic, is very good. They go there to eat. Then they meet Abby and Sarah for a movie. The movie is about a rich lady who gives a concert in New York's Carnegie Hall, even though she can't sing!

1. Where are Shelley and Jenny?
2. Why are they shopping for dresses?
3. Where do they go to eat?
4. Who do they meet for the movie?
5. What is the movie about?

Check for Mastery

1. _____, ask _____ | he / she | what wants to do?
   _____, tell _____ that you have to study because ___.

2. _____, tell _____ that you are going to _____ tonight.
   Ask | him / her | if | he / she | wants to join you.

3. _____, ask _____ what book | he / she | is reading.
   _____, tell ___ that you are reading *War and Peace* for English class.

4. _____, ask _____ what *Adventure Time* is about.
   ___, tell | him / her | you like *Adventure Time* because___

5. ___, ask ___ to come to your house at 8:00 tonight.
   _____, thank | him / her | but say that you need to study.

Chapter 10: Review Your Progress

Speeches

Directions: Choose one of the topics below and prepare a speech that answers the questions.

1. Going to the movies

>When are you going?
>
>Who's going with you?
>
>What time will you meet?
>
>What movie will you see?
>
>What have you heard about the movie?

2. My Family

>How many brothers and sisters do you have?
>
>What are their names?
>
>Who is the oldest? The youngest?
>
>Where does your family live?
>
>How many cousins do you have?
>
>Do they live near you or far away?

3. About Myself

What's your name? Your last name?

How old are you?

Where do you live?

What time do you leave to go to class?

What do you like to do after class?

What do you do in the evenings?

What food do you like?

4. Friends

Who is your best friend?

What is he/she like?

Where does he/she live?

Is his/her house far from here?

What do you do together?

5. My Day

Tell about a typical day for you, from morning until night.

Writing

Directions: Write about one of the topics below. Then read your story to your partner. Ask your partner to help you edit your story. Listen to your partner's story and help him/her edit his/her story.

1. A funny day

2. My favorite class

3. Why I don't like to _____

4. My favorite uncle/brother/cousin/sister

5. What I like to do for free time

6. My favorite TV shows

7. I would like to _____

Student Notes

Note to Teachers

This book is designed to give English learners FLUENCY and FLEXIBILITY in everyday conversations, providing a solid foundation for academic learning in reading and writing English. It is based on the audio-lingual approach used by the U.S. Foreign service for rapid acquisition of foreign languages such as Spanish.

I have applied the same process to students learning English. By the end of this book, your students will be able to engage in everyday conversations with fluency and confidence.

Each lesson is composed of the following instructional routines:

1. **Listen to Conversations.** You will need to record native English speakers, speaking at a normal rate and with appropriate expression, for this segment. Students will listen to English conversational routines while also viewing their native language (Spanish in this edition). Repeating this segment at the beginning of each class session will help them "tune their ears" to native English pronunciations and rhythms.

2. **Learn Sentence Patterns.** This is the part of the lesson that will help English learners become automatic on listening and speaking. Lead your students through each conversational routine using the Gradual Release of Responsibility model:

1. **My turn.** Model the sentence or question, using the first choice in the text box. For example, "Hello, **Alexis**. What's up? How are you?"
2. **Together.** Have students repeat with you.
3. **Your turn.** Have students read to each other.

At this point, give the students the next selection in the text box. For example, **Marcela.** Their job is to repeat the conversational routine, substituting Marcela for Alexis.

If you can enlist a native English speaker as a co-teacher for the first lesson, you can model for students what you want them to do.

It is important to keep the pace of your conversational routines at or very close to native English speaking.

Repeat each oral drill as often as needed to help English learners master these conversational turn-taking routines. They should be able to participate in these turn-taking drills without hesitancy or mispronunciations, with near-native prosody.

3. **Practice Questions and Answers.** This provides additional practice with the major conversational routines of the lesson. Depending on how fluently your students mastered the basic drills, you may either continue to use "I Read, We Read, You Read" or simply have them read to each other.

4. **Practice with Partners.** In this conversational practice routine, students will engage in actual conversation by substituting their own and their partner's names and response choices. For example, when one asks "How are you?" the other will respond with their personal choice: "fine, so so, better, much better."

5. **Review.** This is a brief review of the conversational routines of the chapter. In the beginning these are reading reviews. Later, students will be asked to respond in writing.

6. **Check for Mastery.** This is the part of the lesson where you can assess your students' mastery of the conversational routines of the chapter. In this part you will ask a student to engage in a conversational routine with another student. For example: "_____, ask _____ how he/she is." This requires the student to change the verb form from third person singular to second person singular in order to respond: "_____, how are you?"

Perhaps at this point you're wondering where the grammar lessons are, especially since I mentioned "third person singular" and "second person singular." Grammar TIPS are included when appropriate, for example, to explain that English does not have the formal and informal manner of addressing other people. But the brain learns by patterns, not rules, and this method focuses on establishing patterns of language on the path to full mastery of English receptive and expressive language.

You may want to develop grammar lessons AFTER students have mastered a particular conversational routine. For example, in my Spanish I class, I taught students how to conjugate regular Spanish verbs, e.g. hablar, after they had practiced them in conversational routines. I found this to be far superior to the way that I had learned Spanish, and to the method of the Spanish II, III, and IV classes that I inherited. At the end of the year, my first-year Spanish students were far ahead of the students in my advanced courses in speaking and writing connected discourse.

Whether you are using this book to teach English learners in a Spanish-speaking country or those who are newcomers to the United States, you will also want to supplement this book with print and digital materials that introduce your students to the cultural and contextual surroundings of the conversational routines that they are learning. The following ADDITIONAL RESOURCES section lists books that provide visual and textual reinforcement for the lessons in this book.

Additional Resources

The following resources will amplify the effect of your conversation lessons by providing visual and cultural information to your new English speakers:

Adelson-Goldstein, J., & Shapiro, N. (2008). *Monolingual Oxford Picture Dictionary: Second Edition.* New York: Oxford University Press.

This picture dictionary, designed for adults, contains a plethora of pictures on important topics for newcomers: Everyday language people, housing, food, clothing, health, community, transportation, and work. Besides individual thumbnail pictures with labels, each chapter has a large picture of an environment or event, accompanied by questions about the scene, a short story to read, and questions to think about. For example, "A Family Reunion" asks students to count how many relatives are in the picture and to identify the children who are misbehaving.

This book would also be suitable for middle and high-school newcomers to the U.S. In addition, it could serve as an inspiration for student-developed picture dictionaries of hand-drawn or digital images retreived from the internet that correspond to each of the chapters in *Conversational English for Spanish Speakers.*

Short, D., Tinajero, J., Alfred, T., Moore, D., & Bernabei, G. (2009). *Inside the U.S.A.* National Geographic Learning.

Available through Engage Learning (http://www.cengage.com/), this textbook is designed for newcomer students in middle and high school. I think it would also be an appropriate resource in an adult ESL program. This text introduces U.S. culture while teaching essential vocabulary, language functions, reading, and writing. Many units reinforce the language routines that students learn in *Conversational English for Spanish Speakers.* It does not, however, provide the intensive practice in speaking and listening that is the focus of my book. So my advice would be to pair the chapters of this conversation book with corresponding chapters in *Inside the U.S.A.* There is also an accompanying student workbook.

LaGrone, G., McHenry, A., & O'Connor, P. (1961). *Espanol: Entender y Hablar.* New York: Holt, Reinhart and Winston.

I would be remiss in not mentioning the audio-lingual Spanish I textbook that I used with my high-school students on my return to the U.S. It is, of course, written for English-speaking students who are learning Spanish. However, if you are able to find a used copy, it may provide additional inspiration for your work with newcomers to the English language.

Dedication

This book is dedicated to the people who inspired it: The students of the Bolivian college that I visited, *La Universidad Academica Catolica,* and their ESL teacher, Aubrey Kimble. After watching the students struggle with formulating English questions and answers about parts of the body despite their teacher's creative lesson, I wrote a conversational English lesson on a real-wold topic: "Illnesses and Accidents."

When Aubrey and I introduced the pattern drills to the students, they derided them as "high school." But they gamely gave it a try, and by the end of the class period it was obvious that this was the approach that they needed for English fluency. This book represents the culmination of my work in the peaceful mountain environment of Carmen Pampa, pictured below as our U.S. students said goodbye to their Bolivian friends.

Printed in the USA
CPSIA information can be obtained
at www.ICGtesting.com
LVHW020547180923
758485LV00009B/696